Little Lamb Pho

Poems to make Phonics f-u-n!

By Jude Lennon and Claire Chrystall

www.teamauthoruk.co.uk

About the Author

Jude Lennon is a former Early Years teacher turned Storyteller (Little Lamb Tales) and children's writer. She is the current Disney Winnie the Pooh Laureate for the North West.

Encouraged by Gerard Durcan (the Headteacher from a school Jude worked at in London), Jude wrote this collection of poems to tie in with Phases 2, 3 and 5 of Letters and Sounds. They proved an instant hit with her class and made phonic sessions more enjoyable for everyone.

The poems were illustrated by Claire Chrystall and put onto a CDRom resource complete with word cards, caption cards and Signalong actions for each of the sounds taught. This CD resource is still available from Jude's website. All the poems are now available together in this book.

Jude has also written several children's books including
The Dragon of Allerton Oak
The Toffee Lady - a special commission for Everton Football Club
Astronaut Lamby
Super Bob - a special commission for The Slow Down For Bobby Trust
Glad To Be Dan - a mindfulness book for children with Jo Howarth
Am I Nearly There Yet? - a bilingual picture book with Kelly Thornhill

For more information about Jude's storytelling, books or phonic training please see www.littlelambpublishing.co.uk
or facebook.com/JudeLennonAuthor
facebook.com/Littlelambphonics
facebook.com/Littlelambtales

About the Illustrator

Claire is a Liverpool based artist working as a freelance illustrator from her studio in the beautiful Bluecoat Arts Centre.

In recent years she has specialised in illustrating children's books. Inspiration for her work, coming from Richard Scary, Judith Kerr and Eric Carle amongst many renowned children's illustrators.

Claire has worked on diverse projects from soundbooks for Ladybird Publishing to educational books, children's magazines, and for Girl Guiding UK producing illustrations for the Brownies and Rainbows.

Over the years, Claire has worked alongside numerous clients, both nationally and internationally, on a wide range of products. Her illustrations of square cows and dancing chickens were used to decorate mugs and trays for Marks and Spencer, her leaping frogs for Superdrug, and dancing cows for Anchor butter. Claire's artwork has also been used to enhance party cakes, wrapping paper, greetings cards, teapots, tea towels, tablecloths, placemats, clocks, beach towels and calendars.

Claire's work has a broad appeal especially to young children with strong colours and fun characters. If you would like any further information, please email her at claire_chrystall@hotmail.com

You can view many examples of Claire's work at
www.childrensillustrators.com/clairechrystall
And follow her on Twitter @clairechrystall

Contents Page

The order in which the sounds are taught is not alphabetical. Teaching children the sounds in this way enables them to read and spell simple words with only a very few letters. These letters are then built upon over the weeks and are taught in the following order.

Phase

Two

 **Ss**

Six sausages sizzle in the pan.
They hiss, spit and crackle before they bang!
Six sausages splattered on the pan.
No sausages for tea - so what's the plan?

 Aa

An ant and an alligator came to tea.
An ant and an alligator sat down with me.
The ant had avocado and eggs and ham.
The alligator had apples, jelly and jam.
An ant and an alligator came to tea.
I wonder what they thought of me.

 Tt

Ten tiny teddies all dressed in red,
Tiptoed up to their tiny teddy beds.
Ten tiny teddies lay down their heads.
And fell fast asleep in their tiny teddy beds.

 Ii

A big, itchy insect went to India one day.
The big, itchy insect wanted to stay.
The big, itchy insect is happy to be,
Living in India with you and me.

 **Pp**

Popping popcorn – Pop! Pop! Pop!
Put it in a pan with the lid on top.
Pick up the lid and peep inside...
Popping popcorn – Pop! Pop! Pop!

 Nn

My Nan took Nina and I for tea.
We nibbled nuts – they were yummy.
Nina had nine nuts and I had three.
Nina was full – no room for her tea!

 **Mm**

Mud can be slimy,
It's all over me!
Mud makes great mud pies –
I'm sure you'll agree!

Mud is marvellous.
Mud makes me laugh.
Mud makes me messy.
Mud in my bath!

 Dd

Dig, dig, Daisy Dog,
Deep in the ground.
Dig, dig, Daisy Dog,
What have you found?
Dig, dig, Daisy Dog,
A big juicy bone.
Dig, dig, Daisy Dog,
Gobble it down!

 Gg

Green eggs,
Green cheese,
Grey spaghetti,
Grey peas!

Golden steak,
Golden ham,
Grim dinner,
Grim jam.

I really am a terrible cook.
I must get lessons from a book!

 Oo

Off you go Mr Otter,
On your way!
Octopus is coming to stay.
I've bought some oranges and olives to eat.
Octopus loves them as a treat.

Off you go Mr Otter,
On your way!
Ostrich is coming to take you away.
His friend Orang-utan is coming too.
A wonderful time will be had by you!

Cc

Hector is a cuddly cat.
Hector is a cute cat.
Victor is a clever cat.
Victor is a climbing cat.

Hector likes Victor.
Victor likes Hector.
Two cute cats can play together!
Meow!

 Kk

A tiny kitten found a great big key!
It belonged to the Duke of Kent, you see.
The kitten picked up the enormous key,
And returned it to the Duke at three.
"Oh Thank you," said the Duke with glee.
"Won't you come and live with me?"

 **ck**

Tick-tock, tick-tock, goes the clock.
It's time to get up quick, quick, quick!

Put on your clothes and your shoes and socks.
Brush your teeth, you'd better be quick!

Pick up your coat, your hat and your pack.
Now be on your way and don't be late back!

 Ee

Eggs with legs!
Eggs in beds!
Eggs with pegs!
Eggs in sheds!

I love eggs -
Eggs are the best!

 Uu

A muffin to eat.
A mug of tea.
A hug from Mum.
A hug for me.

"Now, under the covers.
I'll shut the door.
Go to sleep.
I'll be up to make sure!"

 **Rr**

My rabbit called Rod eats carrots for his tea.
My rabbit called Rod is furry as can be.
My rabbit called Rod, so cute and fluffy.
My rabbit called Rod really loves me!

 **Hh**

Henry has a hat on his head.
Henry's hat is big and red.
Henry wears it everywhere...
Even when he's in his bed!

 **Bb**

Big, blue, bouncy ball,
Bounced down the street.
Big, blue, bouncy ball,
Bounced to the beach.
Big, blue, bouncy ball,
Bounced to the park.
Big, blue, bouncy ball,
Squashed by a car!

POP

 Ff

A fat fish met a flat fish, swimming in the sea.
The flat fish asked the fat fish to come for tea.
"I only eat figs and French fries" said he.
"Well I've plenty of those – just come and see!"

 **ff**

Fluffy eats all kinds of stuff.
He even ate Dad's cuffs today.
Dad was in a terrible huff.
Fluffy didn't care and went off to play.

Ll

Licking lollies is lovely and yummy.
Licking lamposts is silly and funny!
Give me a lolly to lick any day.
And leave the lamposts to light the way!

11

I threw a ball to my mate Nell.
She dropped it, and to the floor it fell.
The ball rolled away and Nell gave a yell.
"Oh no! It's fallen down the well!"

ss

"Miss Moss, Miss Moss, I think you'll be cross!

I've got paint and glue all over my dress.

Miss Moss, Miss Moss, I think you'll be cross!

It really is a terrible mess!"

But Miss Moss came and cleared the mess,

She dried my eyes and said "Don't fuss."

She cleaned the paint and glue from my dress.

"Ah thanks Miss Moss, you are the best!"

Phase

Three

Jj

Jellyfish like juggling.
Jellyfish like jam.
Jellyfish like jogging.
Jellyfish like ham.

Jellyfish like pyjamas.
Jellyfish like hiding.
Jellyfish like jelly.
But mostly, they like jiving!

Vv

A violin in a vase?
That's not right!
A violin in a vase?
What a sight!
Violins make music, I've been told.
And a vase holds violets, lovely and bold!

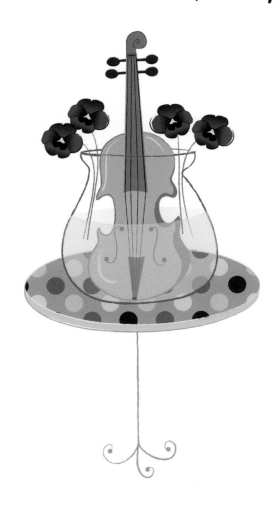

 **Ww**

Wet weather.
Windy weather.
Winter weather.
Warm weather.

Which weather will it be?
Open the window and you will and see!

 Xx

A fox, in a box, in a terrible fix!
The ox has stolen his Pick and Mix.

"You naughty ox," shouted Mr Fox.
"You should know better, you're nearly six!"

 # Yy

Yellow yo-yo, down you go.

Yellow yo-yo, up you flow.

Yellow yo-yo, up and down.

Yellow yo-yo, on the ground!

Yellow yo-yo needs a rest.

So I will eat a yoghurt next!

 **Zz**

Zippy Zebra lived in a zoo.
Zippy Zebra wished he was blue.
One day, a wizard came whizzing through.
Azacazam! Zippy's wish came true!

zz

Fizzy the Fly felt dizzy and sick.

He'd been twizzling around with his best mate Rick.

Fizzy buzzed back to his little fuzzy tree.

The rain drizzled down and he fell fast asleep.

A blizzard came and swirled around.

But Fizzy was snoring and heard not a sound!

 Qq (qu)

Quick!
It's the queen!
Quick!
She might see.
Quick!
Make it tidy.
Quick!
Make it clean.

Uh oh, too late,
She's here, she's seen.
The quarrelsome queen is going to be mean!

ch

Cheese on chips,
Cheese on chops,
Cheese on chicken,
Cheese on chocs.

Cheese for brunch,
Cheese for lunch,
Cheese to munch,
Cheese to crunch.

Cheese is funny,
Cheese is scrummy,
Cheese is yummy.
Look out tummy!

sh

Shiny, silver shells
Sitting on the shore.
Shiny, silver shells
I wish I had you all.

Shiny, silver shells
Please come home with me.
Shiny, silver shells,
Washed by the sea.

 th/th

This feather is white.
This feather is black.
This feather is thin.
And this one is fat.

This feather is short.
This feather is long.
They belong to the thrushes.
Listen to their song.

♪ ng

I love to sing a song,
Especially when I'm swimming!

I love to bang a drum,
Especially when I'm marching.

I love to spread my wings,
Especially when I'm flying!

I love doing lots of things.
My favourite thing is laughing!

 ai

Rain, rain, you are a pain,

As welcome as a dirty stain!

Rain, rain, disappear.

Splash and gurgle down the drain!

 **ee**

A bee in a tree had hurt his knee.
"I need a doctor to come and see!"

The doctor came and looked at the knee.
"You're fine Mr Bee, go back to your tree!"

 **igh**

Lovely knight, won't you fight,
the big, fierce dragon with all your might?
He comes and scares me in the night.
He really is a terrible sight!

Princess don't worry, by morning light,
the dragon will be gone and the world will be bright.
I'll fight him and beat him with all my might.
And we shall be married the very next night!

oa

A goat in a coat,
Got into a boat.
The goat in the boat
Started to float.
The goat in the coat
Stood up in the boat.
And then he fell in
And was soaked to the skin!

Silly goat!

 oo (short)

Robin Hood lived in a wood.
The people thought he was very good.
The Sheriff stole their silver and gold.
So Robin Hood made a plan that was bold!

He hid in the woods as the Sheriff rode by.
And he grabbed the gold in the blink of an eye!
Robin Hood had saved the day.
"Good old Robin, Hip, Hip, Hooray!"

 oo (long)

My big balloon took me up to the moon.
Where I met an alien whose name was Boon.

Boon showed me around with his pet named Froon.
He even gave me an alien spoon.

But all too soon it was time to zoom.
So it's bye to Boon and his little pet Froon.

 ar

I caught a star
And put it in a jar.
I took my star
For a drive in my car.
I drove the star
Away so far,
And set it free
To fly afar!

or

I used a fork to eat some corn.
The corn was just like dry old cork.
Can I have something else for tea?
Torn pork will do, it is yummy!

 ur

I burnt my hand.
It really hurt!
Enough to make my hair curl!

I burnt my hand.
The blister burst!
And splurted out with a great big spurt!

Yuck!

ow

Wow! A cow who lives in a tower.

Wow! A cow with amazing power!

Wow! A cow holding a flower.

Wow! A cow in a power shower!

oi

Come and join me in the soil.

Let's dig deep, we might find oil.

Come and join me, help me toil,

Let's find the coins in the soil.

Come and join me in the soil.

What's that you've found?

A bit of tinfoil!

ear

What can you hear with your little ear?

It's something loud and it's getting near!

What can you hear with your little ear?

It's something horrible that is clear!

What can you hear with your little ear?

Is it a monster getting near?

If so, I will cry lots of tears.

A big, bad monster is what I fear!

 air

Here comes the fairy with golden fair hair.
Here comes the fairy, floating in the air.
Here comes the fairy with golden fair hair.
She lives in the forest in her fairy lair.

 ure

This manure sure does smell!
I feel quite unwell.

Pure roses would do,
And daisies as well.

I just need a cure for this terrible smell.
Surely it's something the chemist would sell?

er

A runner needs water to run much faster.
A walker needs water to walk for longer.
A flower needs water to grow much taller.
We all need water – it makes us stronger!

Phase Five

 ay

Today is the perfect day to say
"Let's all go to the park and play."

We'll feed the ducks and play in the sand.
"May I have an ice cream, one in each hand?"

Today is the perfect day to say
"Let's be on our way to the park to play."

 ou

The cloud floats gently without a sound.
Hovering way up, above the ground.
The cloud keeps still and I have found.
It's the earth that keeps on turning around.

 ie

A tie in a pie?
Surely not!
A tie gets tied around your neck in a knot.

A tie in a pie?
It can't be true!
Someone has told a lie to you!

 ea

I'm weak, I'm weak!
I'm going to eat
Lots of lovely, juicy meat.

I'll eat my feast
on this neat seat.
It is a truly lovely treat!

oy

A boy called Roy needed new toys.

His others were broken by some boys.

Roy was very annoyed with the boys.

"Oy! That's not fair, you've destroyed my toys!"

The boys said sorry and gave Roy some new toys.

So Roy wasnt annoyed, he was filled with joy!

A skirt in twirly paper.
A shirt from Uncle Ray.
A birthday girl's presents.
She's thirteen today.

ue

A barbecue is great, it's true.
But I'm always at the back of the queue.

So next time, when the sky is blue.
I'll be up early and in front of Sue.

aw

I saw a paw print on the lawn,
Sparkling in the frosty dawn.
It looked so pretty, I had to draw,
The paw print twinkling on the lawn.

wh

Where are you going?
What will you see?
When are you setting off?
When you've had your tea?

Which way are you going?
Who is going too?
When you're ready,
Can I come too?

ph

I took a photo on my phone,
Of the Pharaoh of Egypt on his throne.
The pharaoh looked at the photo and said.
"My phone is better, use that instead!"

ew

Let's have a brew – and share our news.
Let's have a brew and chew the fat.
Let's have a brew and a bowl of stew.
It's a little bit chewy – sorry about that!

 oe

A doe found some potatoes in a wood.
They dropped on her toes where she stood.
The doe looked down at her sore little toes.
"My toes are all squashed, just like tomatoes!"

au

At the end of August, it's Autumn,
A perfect time to write.
I want to be an author.
On that I've set my sights.

Automobiles covered in sauce.
My friends - Laura, Maude and Saul.
Haunted towers and a dragon's den.
They'll all come out of this author's pen!

ey

A monkey was walking in a valley one day.

He met a donkey who started to say

"I'm having a picnic, would you like to come?

There's lots of food to fill your tum.

Smokey roast turkey with lashings of honey.

Delicious and yet, it won't cost any money.

Please say you'll come, it will be such fun."

The monkey was starving and set off at a run!

 a-e

Can you bake me a cake with grapes and dates?
Can you make me a cake in the shape of a snake?
Can you bake me a cake that looks like a name?
It's for my best friend, his name is James.

 e-e

These are my friends who live in Crete.
Steve, Eve and don't forget Pete.
Steve completes crosswords.
Eve likes Chinese.
Pete just loves Crete, it makes him complete!

 i-e

I like the ice, it's smooth and it shines.
I like the ice to glide and slide.
I like the ice, it makes me smile.
But I don't like falling on my side!

 o-e

I went to the woods, I was all alone.

I found a really magic stone.

It took me to the witch's home.

Smoke was pouring from her stove.

She looked at me and I just froze.

She said she'd make stew from my bones.

I screamed "No Way !" and with that I fled.

And then I woke up in my comfy bed!

The duke gave a silver flute to June.
She used it daily to make a tune.
But her flute was really not quite right.
It was shaped like a cube, not a tube in sight!

Activities for Parents to try

1. Read a chosen poem and talk about the sound the letter or letters make.

2. Identify objects in the illustration that start with or contain the sound you are focusing on.

3. Identify the words containing that sound throughout the poem.

4. Go on an object hunt around your house/garden to find objects beginning with the sound or containing the sound.

5. Play I spy but say the sound rather than the letter name.

6. Use magnetic letters or floating letters to make words containing the sound from the poem.

7. Try to come up with a silly sentence using the sound from the poem.

8. Read and share books and stories every day.

Activities for Schools

Here are some activities you can use in Phonics sessions in school. Have fun!

1. Musical Letters - put on some music, dance around the space you have. When the music stops, hold up a grapheme/digraph/trigraph and ask children to make the correct sound.

2. Stations Game - this is a hugely versatile game that can be used for many subjects. For phonics, fill a bag with a mixed selection of objects/words. Place four different graphemes/digraphs/trigraphs in each corner of the room. Dig in the bag, pull out an object/word and ask children run to the correct place. As children get more confident simply call out words for them to run to the correct place. The children can take the teacher role too.

3. Pegging letters - string up a washing line and using a collection of up to six letters let children make as many words as they can from the letters they have in 30 seconds. The children take it in turn to make a word each. As children get more confident they can write down a list of the words they make.

4. Treasure Hunt - hide objects around the space (this can be done indoors or outdoors). If outdoors, chalk large graphemes/digraphs/trigraphs on the floor, if indoor place large graphemes/digraphs/trigraphs in each corner). Ask children to search the space and bring their treasure back before putting it in the right place.

5. Word Hunt - using two soft toys and two different sounds, hide words around the classroom. Ask children to work in pairs to go and find two words. When they bring them back they must decide which soft toy gets their words. You can add some red herrings too. Check the answers are right.

6. Caption Bingo - you'll need two sets of matching captions containing words with the sound you are learning. (These are available on my CDRom resource). Split the group in two and sit them in two rows facing one another. One child reads out their caption and the child with the matching caption holds it up and says BINGO! This can be done with words or letters too.

7. Word Match - this is a good one for 'Tricky' words and can be done with the whole class. Give out a selection of tricky words (you'll need at least four of each word), and ask children to find all the other people with the same word as them. When this is done, ask each group to come up with a sentence containing their word.

8. Pass the Tin - fill a tin or box with a selection of objects that start with your given sound. Add a few red herrings. Place a copy of the sound you've chosen on the floor in the middle of the circle. Pass the tin around the circle. I use the tune London Bridge and sing "Take the tin and pass it round, pass it round, pass it round, take the tin and pass it round, choose something when it stops!" At the end of the rhyme the child with the tin chooses an object. If the object starts with your given sound place it on top of the grapheme/digraph/trigraph.

9. Disco Letters - give out a selection of graphemes/digraphs/trigraphs (you'll need four copies of each one you use). Play the music. When it stops, children must find everyone who has the same as them. This can be done with words too.

10. Fruit Salad - this game can be used for letters/words/captions. Choose four letters/words/captions and give these out around the circle. Call one out and the children with that letter/word or caption must swap places with the other children who have the same.

Printed in Great Britain
by Amazon